My Many Years

My Many Years

Mary Lou Nance Ivey

Copyright © 2009 by Mary Lou Nance Ivey.

Library of Congress Control Number: 2009906757
ISBN: Hardcover   978-1-4415-5185-6
               Softcover   978-1-4415-5184-9

All rights reserved. No part of this book may be reproduced or transmitted in any form or by any means, electronic or mechanical, including photocopying, recording, or by any information storage and retrieval system, without permission in writing from the copyright owner.

This book was printed in the United States of America.

To order additional copies of this book, contact:
Xlibris Corporation
1-888-795-4274
www.Xlibris.com
Orders@Xlibris.com

CONTENTS

The Clock 13
My Days 14
When We Were Kids 15
My Life 16
The Past 18
Old Time Memories 19
Getting Older 20
Then and Now 21
Which Of These? 23
Fifty 24
A Rhyme Full of Love 26
Mary Magdalene 28
Dear Lady 29
Thank You, My Lady 30
Shunning Nationalities 31
God's People 32
Darlene 34
My Aunt Caroline 35
A Rainbow 36
My Uncle Bill 37
Letter Writing 38
Aunt Caroline 39
No Letter Today 40
The Sky 42
Souls 44
Dear Alexa 45
Alexa 46
Forgiveness 47
Our Home 48
A Little Baby 50
You Are A Mother 51
God In All 52

Blessings	53
Contempt Vs. Love	54
Just A Prayer	55
Seal Of Friendship	56
Kindness	57
Please	58
Jim Nance's "Sadie"	59
A Friend	60
The Sweet Old Lady	61
What Is Real?	62
Eternity	63
Sins	64
Prayer Problems	65
Rights Of The Road	66
Those Bulletins	67
Sanctifying Grace	68
Grandma	69
Go To Him	70
Grazing Time	71
Thank Him	72
A Narrow Line	73
God's Gentle Rain	74
Tommy	75
Jerry	76
God's Loved Ones	77
The Waiting Room	78
Our Future	79
Monsignor Burns	80
John Paul II	81
Love Wishes	82
The Beauty Shop	83
Legs	85
Thank You, Lord	86
Often	87
Carry On	88
Popcorn	89
My Valentine	90
Think About It . . .	91
My Love	92

He Isn't You	93
Needs	94
Sunday Morning	95
The Mountains	96
The Christian Way	97
St. Patrick's Day	98
Each Day I Pray	99
Did'ja	100
Compassion	101
Nature	102
Jelly-N-Me	104
Time	105
Thanksgiving	106
Instead	107
My Dog Penny	108
No One	109
God's Helpers	110
A Prayer	111
Oma	112
Lucky Me	113
The Rights Of Others	114
George West	115
A Daughter	116
Albert	117
The End	118
Gossip	119
Your Way	120
The Dance Floor	121
My Angel "Butch"	122
Smile	123
My "Danny Boy"	124
Love Is Important	125
I Love You, Jesus	126
The White Clouds	127
Harold	128
Memory Of Alzheimer's	129
Lonely Or Blue	130
A Priest	131
A Cowboy	132

The Unused Rule	133
White-Clothed Nuns	134
Sleepless Nights	135
Want	136
T.V.	137
The Old Fashioned Clothesline	139
A Working Mother	140
Daddy	141
A Letter To Jesus	143
Holy Innocents	144
An Abortion	146
A Wife	147
Wedding Bells	148
If Husbands **Really** Want A Happy Marriage	149
My Darling Eileen	150
Ellen	151
Carrie	152
Grandfather	153
The Wrong Hand	154
Those Mothballs	155
Grandpa's Hands	156
All Night Adoration	157
You	158
Anticipation	159
My Husband	160
'My' God	161
What To Do	162
He Loved Me Anyway	163
Death Is Beautiful	164

THE CLOCK

In 1970 I designed a clock with no numbers, just faces. No one understood what I wanted until 1980, when my son Tommy's best friend became a photographer—Frank made my clock.

The wood alone was over $100. Frank took the pictures. Instead of #1, there was a picture of my first born, Ann. Instead of #2 there was a picture of my second born, Peggy. Then Tommy my third child and so on. Since we ONLY had 11 children, Tom and I were 12 o'clock.

All of the children wanted the clock but Wayne was the first of the grandchildren to ask, so it's his, when I die, of course.

THE CLOCK

Each time a clock chimes hours
Or ticks minutes in a day
I know sweet Lord that it's Your will
That time will pass away.

At one o'clock I see my Ann
At two it's Peggy's face
At three o'clock my Tommy love
And Danny's in fourth place

At five o'clock my lovely Nora
Colleen's there at six
My precious Jerry's number seven
Eileen's where the eight is fixed

And lovely red-heads nine and ten
Are Ellen and Maura Jo
With number eleven coming last
We all call him Jim Bo.

Tom and I will take last place
"Our hours" have almost gone
But life continues on each day
Our children's lives will carry on.

1980

MY DAYS

1926 was the year I was born
Not too many folks old as me
The depression came and we were the same
`cept we were poor as we could be.

We were hungry a lot, but most of us got
through bad times and through good
We knew God was there, and He would share
the fruits and things that He could.

When the war came we still were kids
though many friends went to fight
So many were killed, but the brave things they did
Gave us courage and our country delight.

That's far in the past & more wars in between
Our God still leading our way.
I may be old, but the stories be told
not many have seen my day.

April 4, 2006

WHEN WE WERE KIDS

There was no money to fight about
Money! What was that?
There were no toys for us to share
Except a ball and bat.

And when "WE" played baseball
I was never on the team
No one ever chose me
It seemed so very mean!

I couldn't throw, I couldn't hit
I couldn't even run
I just wanted to be with you
It seemed like so much fun.

We all have made mistakes in life
That is very clear
As long as we return to God
There is no need to fear.

Now we're in our GOLDEN YEARS
What on earth is that?
We've lost our memories, some our minds,
We're too thin or way too fat.

The young folks don't realize
We are a wealth of knowledge
I still can't throw or hit a ball
But I could help someone to college.

The years gone by, for some of us,
Can bring a lot of pleasure
As long as we say kind works
For THAT is how God measures.

July 24, 1995

MY LIFE

It seems so long since I was wed
When I was very young—
Eager to please, anxious to do,
For me, life'd just begun.

Our home I kept neat, our babies kept clean,
My God, I kept plainly in sight;
For all of my tasks—happy or not
I tried to fulfill with delight.

Experience slowly had come with the years,
Unhappiness sometimes too;
But remembering God would stay by my side
Always brought courage anew.

Temptation has come—and quite often sin—
I'm thankful that God is my Judge!
No man on this earth would forgive as "He" does
And help back with so gentle a nudge.

Accepting God's will—when it isn't mine
Has been the hardest to do—
Material things mean none to my soul
And my heart knows when I've been true.

I feel so very tired—
How much longer must I stay?
Do you think that I might come in June
Or even sooner—May?

I feel so very useless—
to my family and to friends
Is there something I still can do
Before my life shall end?

If only I have taught my girls—
And even helped my boys,
My life shall not have been in vain
And life for them be filled with joy.

August 21, 1971

THE PAST

We all dream of years gone by . . .
Especially the old
They remember pleasant things . . .
Stories never told!

The happiness when they were loved
And looked their very best
But when you're old and wrinkled
Youth would not have guessed.

Look to the years, when they were young
And worked so very fast
But youth today—cannot convey
To look into the past.

Very soon the youth of "now"
Will be the "old" of then,
They'll look back remembering
For it's the fate of men

June 1980

OLD TIME MEMORIES

Can you imagine falling
Up instead of down
Have you ever seen a face
Only with a frown?
A smile is so much better—
Kindly thoughts help too
You feel like love's all 'round you
No matter what you do.

Even when you're older
And "some" don't want you 'round
Your memory takes you to a place
And doesn't make a sound.
The happy times when you were young
No one can erase
Many keep them in their hearts—
You can see it in their face.

The young are really "captured"
With tales about the past
Help them store up memories
And love to hold them fast
Help them know about our God
Who's waiting for us all
He even sent us angels
To help if we should fall.

I've often heard that "youth"
Is wasted on the young
What a silly statement—
Their lives have just begun.

October 5, 1998

GETTING OLDER

I know I'm getting older
But so is everyone.
Fingers bending—pain is sending
We can't have a lot of fun.

But after all the pain
That our Lord went through
We dare not complain
"He" suffered for me & you.

We must thank Him for our pain
Remembering it's free
It's our 'Key to Heaven'
It opens up for you & me.

June 20, 2008

THEN AND NOW

The "woodshed" isn't standing
As it did in days gone by
The "hickory stick," too, is gone—
We tell this with a sigh
But the closeness of the families
Is what we really miss
The day would start and evening close
With a gentle kiss.

Today it seems like no one cares
Where the other's gone
With the gossip and TV
Life just goes on and on
But see the little child there
As tears run down her face
All she wants in this life
Is love and an embrace.

We cannot live without our God
And love is next in line
Without these, it matters not
If the sun should shine!
Gossip's always bad for you
And TV's often worse
Let our God be our guide
And Mary be our Nurse.

July 13, 1998

WHICH OF THESE?

On January 22, 1973 the 'Abortion Law' was passed. It broke my heart knowing people could KILL their own babies even before they were born.

For years people had put us down for having so many children, but I didn't care. The fact that I had just turned 36 in September and Jimbo was born in October was the clincher. Eleven children in 15 years. There was no end to problems, but that was part of life.

No one in the world could love their children more than I did and still do That was why I wrote "Which to These."

WHICH OF THESE?

Well now I'm in my forties,
These many years I pride
If I had done as many said
I've have these years to hide.

You see, I've many children
And each of them is great
Would I have loved my God as much
If I had stopped at eight?

I have a grandson from my Colleen
He's precious and alive
But he would not have been here
If I had stopped at five.

At many places Danny sings,
He's just ONE pride to me
He never would have been here
If I had stopped at three.

If Ann were my only child
I could have had much fun,
But look at all the love I'd missed
If I had stopped at one.

Which of these, of all my children
Could I live without today?
Not one of the eleven
No matter what "They" say!

January 22, 1973

FIFTY

Fifty years ago today
I took my first long breath
I hope my parents looked at me
With love and tenderness.

Unhappy memories fill my mind
When I was just a child
Wanting love—not luxury
And loving what was mild.

Here I am in tw'light years
Hoping still for love
But most of what I get each day
Is sent from up above.

September 1976

A RHYME FULL OF LOVE

Several years back when I took sign language and "why" I took it is a story in itself.

There was a woman in the class who was nice to me—until she learned that I had eleven children. Then she wouldn't speak to me unless it was necessary. One day she took her 15 year old daughter with her. While she was talking to the teacher, I was talking with the girl. When she returned to her seat, I told her what a lovely daughter she had. Her reply was "I should have aborted her". I knew the girl heard her and she immediately walked over to her mother—maybe to see if she had understood what she had heard. The mother looked the girl right in her eyes and said: "I wished I had aborted you!" The girl's eyes filled with tears and she turned and ran outside. I looked at the mother and said: "How can you be so cruel and say such a thing?" Her answer was: "It's none of your business!"

I ran out the door and looked for the girl, but never found her. The rest of the day and into the evening, I couldn't get the girl and the pain she was in, out of my mind and heart. That night I wrote a poem FOR a girl I didn't know and pray that some day she may read it.

A RHYME FULL OF LOVE

"There was an old lady who lived in a shoe"
 She had lots of kids—well, I do too.

But when Easter comes, or it's Christmastime
 You bet we enjoy it, for love flows like wine.

I may have more work than others around
 But don't give me pity—God's love I have found.

My heart still goes out to those poor lonely girls
Who learn much too late, they've killed Heaven's pearls.

But God in His goodness, still will reach out
 And fill up His Heaven—with babies, no doubt.

April 1980

MARY MAGDALENE

There were many kids on drugs in the early 70's. Mostly some just trying marijuana because it was something new to them, but it soon became something stronger. I'm ashamed of my generation—mostly because so many of us just gave the kids money to get them out of the house and this, of course, was a red flag for trouble.

Having so many children of my own, and having one out there hanging out in a local park, made me the target to be the liaison between the kids and police. Many of the kids came to talk to me and to get advice. My husband wasn't thrilled with this since some of those kids were bigger than we were, but they were young and scared. Then, too, the police, uniformed and plain clothed, were also in and out.

Tom finally put his foot down and said "no more were to be in our house!" With all of the kids in & out, the only thing that was stolen was my butcher knife—that in itself was a miracle.

After awhile two girls, who had been prostituting themselves for drugs, came to me and asked me who they should pray to—to get out of their situation. I told them and wrote the prayer to Mary Magdalene. Afterward, I sent a copy to the Bishop and asked his opinion. He said it was great, but I had misspelled her name—it's corrected now.

MARY MAGDALENE

You once lived in this great wide world—
Accusations against you often were hurled
   You were by trade, an Adulteress!

Your sinfulness and beauty were widely told
And men in high places bid high to unfold
   So lovely are you, an Adulteress!

You were lavished with riches, oil and silk
Your hair soft and shiny—your skin white as milk
   So easy to love you, an Adulteress!

Then Christ became man and had much to say
But much more than words, He just looked your way
   And you shamed for being, an Adulteress!

You sold all your riches and gave to the poor
Hoping that this would help even the score
   For living the life of an Adulteress!

You followed your Lord when He took up His cross
Please beg of Him now for a blessing to toss
   Down to this earth, to me, an Adulteress!

DEAR LADY

Dear Lady—my Lady,
> Please help me be strong.

I need your help
> Because I've been wrong!

I needed love—
> But it came the wrong way,

Now prayers for forgiveness
> Are all I can say.

God's mercy and love
> Are known in our lands

No matter the sin
> He'll hold out His hands

To lift us up
> When we have heavy hearts

So show us forgiveness
> And get a new start.

And so now, my Lady,
> Please intercede

Between me and my God—
> Thank you for this kind deed!

June 1980

THANK YOU, MY LADY

Thank you, my Lady,
        For hearing my prayer!

One rung up the ladder
        With you standing there—-

To guide and protect me
        As I've asked you to do

To follow your footsteps
        To be kind and true.

I needed your guidance
        As you know so well

Each step I was taking
        Could lead me to hell!

Thank you, my Lady,
        For being my friend

Please stay with me now,
        And on to the end.

I wanted my God—-
        But I chose the wrong path

You helped to protect me
        And guard from His wrath!

So I thank you, sweet Lady,
        Let me not away again

Remind me each day
        To stay clear of sin!

June 1980

SHUNNING NATIONALITIES

I'm proud that I am Irish
My God makes no mistakes
Whether it be heritage
Or planets that He makes.

So many are not happy
They look for one to hate
With all our nationalities
I think our country's great.

Why can't people understand
That God has made us all
The many different colors
The short ones and the tall.

If only love and kindness
Were shared by everyone
There'd be no sad tomorrow
For no one would be shunned.

June 1980

GOD'S PEOPLE

Why all the fuss and complaining
About your neighbor or mine?
America's pride is her people
Their language and customs are fine.

We all had to come from somewhere
Christ came from Heaven above
Down to a young Jewish maiden
Who taught us all about love.

God in His wisdom—knows people
God in His wisdom—knows love
But all of us dumb silly people
Think we must push and shove.

If only we'd live as God's people
And listen to the words of His Son
There could never be hate or dissension
'Cause we'd live as He wants us—as one.

June 1980

DARLENE

By Mary Lou Nance-Ivey

When Darlene was a small child. I went to visit them and Darlene wanted to sleep with me, which was fine with me. Bridgette always slept with her mother.

That night Darlene kicked me more than once, I had just had surgery and was in pain.

The next night I went to bed alone. When I went to get up during the night, I stepped on her—she was sleeping on the floor next to my bed. I leaned down and asked her why she was sleeping on the floor. My heart melted when she answered me. "I love you so much and I want to sleep with you, but I was afraid I might hurt you again, so this is as close as I could be to you."

When a small child tells you words like this and is willing to sleep on the floor to be near you, what can you do but love her?

DARLENE

My darling Darlene is 18 today
So much to tell, we love her that way!

She's fast when she's running
from boys or at track
But kindness and compassion
She does not lack.

She knows that her angel
is there at her side.
No matter the problem
He'll help her decide.

To listen is hard for some of us
that's why things often go wrong
If we'd just pray, things would go our way,
and God would help us stay strong.

Always love,
Oma

March 23, 2006

MY AUNT CAROLINE

My dear Aunt's a saint on earth,
Of this I am sincere!
She's sweet and kind and tolerant
And patient and so dear.

If in trouble, she will help you
When needed—she is there
And when there's no solution—
She goes to God in prayer.

Oh yes, she's really human
With troubles of her own
But from her you'll never hear them—
Not even one small groan.

To be like my Aunt Caroline
Is the goal I want to reach
And when our lives have ended—
To be on Heaven's beach.

June 1980

A RAINBOW

One day I looked toward heaven,
And what did I see in the sky?
Not snow, nor sleet, nor raindrops
But a rainbow up on high!

I'm sure I saw God winking
And a smile was on "His" face
He helped overcome my sadness
with "peace" He did replace.

I used to think that punishment
Was all that God conveyed
But through the years I've known "Him"
I know that's not "His" way.

When my words or actions
Are clumsy as can be
I know He's right there watching
And laughing 'long with me.

There always will be rainbows
And God will be nearby
You see "He's" very close to us
Not just up in the sky!

January 15, 1995

MY UNCLE BILL

My dear Uncle Bill, always so gay—
Since a tiny tot, I remember this way.
A lovely Kathryn he claimed for his bride
All through these years, she stayed at his side.

There were four charming boys so healthy, so strong
When one cloudy morning things seemed to go wrong;
God needed an angel, so He claimed their young son
No sweeter an angel could He have picked from.

But my Uncle Bill, with the grief of this day
Would still stop and chat, and appear to be gay.
He carried his mail, day out and day in—
No matter how tired, he always would grin.

The black man, the white man, he claimed for his friend
And I know that whenever he come to his end—
St. Peter will hold the gates both wide and still
And be proud to shake hands with MY UNCLE BILL.

June 1980

LETTER WRITING

Writing letters' easy
And so rewarding, too,
The news that reaches others
Brings warm thoughts of you.

It really isn't difficult
Though many think it so
Just write things as they happen
Take it nice and slow.

The loved ones who are far away
Appreciate your time
Try to be more generous
Just sharpen up your mind.

So send that word of love today
Let them "feel" your smile
As far as kindness is concerned
You've had it all the while.

June 1980

AUNT CAROLINE

My darling Aunt Caroline
So kind and so sweet
She's sensitive, thoughtful
So gentle and meek.

Though her life's been all giving
She asked naught in return
The welfare of others
Her greatest concern.

Of all of the sorrows
I've seen her maintain
Not once in my life
Did I hear her complain.

With her saintly face,
And her sense of humor
You'd almost believe
She is just a rumor.

But I know firsthand
She's a wonderful pal—
My darling Aunt Caroline
Is that kind 'a gal!

June 1980

NO LETTER TODAY

I've quit writing letters
Now this is a quite a shame
Guess I'm just lazy
This must be the blame

Maybe my age is part
Of what's wrong
My voice now is cracking
Can't sing a song

I find excuses for I don't do
Maybe one day I'll be writing to you

But don't hold your breath
You might turn blue
Just remember that I'm
Always thinking of you.

May 20, 2002

THE SKY

How can anyone see the sky and not think of God?

When I wrote this poem I was thinking of everything 'He' has done for us and given to us.

I think it tells about itself.

THE SKY

When God made all the universe
He held not one thing back
He gave us all that we might share
There's nothing that we lack.

He gave us all—the air we breathe
The birds, the trees, the flowers
He put four seasons in the year
With sunshine, snow or showers.

He made the sky so beautiful
He made the clouds so white
Imaginings can go so far
When you watch this lovely sight.

At times of day, it's different, too,
A painter would not dare—-
With sunrise, or with sunset
It's beauty to compare.

It's as if the sky surrounds us,
And holds us in her arms
Sometimes she beams, sometimes she cries,
Sometimes she really storms.

The child in me appreciates
God's beauty and His love
That's why He crowned this universe
With the blue skies up above.

June 1980

SOULS

This goes with the 'The Sky' like a continence. Again I think it, to, is self-explanatory.

SOULS

After He made the universe
God created human souls
The universe would be a waste
If God had not in mind a goal!

God made us in His image
He gave us all free will
He gave us each a conscience
Yet we sin and hurt Him still!

He sent His Son to redeem us
Who died upon the cross
He reopened the gates of heaven
Was all this a total loss?

A soul is something precious
No one but God can make
So many can't see its value
Or love God back, just for His sake.

Those of us with children
Have many lives to mold
We must give love generously
But not forget the time to scold.

Those who live for the things on earth
Will surely lose their souls
Those who look forward to Heaven
Will have finally reached their goal!

June 1980

DEAR ALEXA . . .

Dear Alexa,

      I think of you often
    And pray for you each night
   And wonder when I'll see you
     So I can hold you tight.

     You are a special child
   And one that I hold dear
     I will always love you,
     When far away or near.

    Please remember always
    That God is on your side
So think and stay close to "Him"
  And your angel be your guide.

      Always love,
      Oma

September 23, 2000

ALEXA

Alexa came to visit them
When she was very small
This tiny babe meant so much
To 'Mama Rose' and Jim, so tall.

Her fingers were so tiny
But she wrapped them anyway
Around the hearts of both of them
And they love her more each day.

As the years have come and gone
Their love remains the same
Her curly hair and pretty eyes
Tells that this is not a game.

Alexa and now Jasmine
Are sweet as they can be
I hope that they will always love
A grandma just like me.

June 19, 2001

FORGIVENESS

Forgiveness can take any hate away
It can also take away greed
It can help take the doubts that fill your mind
It can prove it's love that you need

Don't keep bad feelings within you
It will eat up your life and your mind
Remember God suffered, more then you know
Yet it's only His love that you find

Jealousy and self-pity will harm you
Don't let them take over your life
You need to forgive those who hurt you
Or you'll pain like the blade of a knife.

May 6, 1996

OUR HOME

I looked the whole world over
And what do you think I saw?
A place in our great nation
A home with many a flaw.

It's seen happiness and sadness
Health and sickness, too,
It's held many little children
Who belonged to me and you.

I've often said, "I'm leaving"
But never took a step
To leave this home with memories
Where I'd so often wept.

I thank my God—for, oh so much—
For kindness and for fear
I thank Him for our "lived in home"
Want to say, "I'm glad we're here!"

February 3, 1974

A LITTLE BABY

Whenever I think of the poem 'Which of These'. I also think of a 'little baby'. How can anyone not love a little baby? They are so precious so trusting, so innocent. This is not what I planned to write when I started this, but I'm glad it was what I did write.

A LITTLE BABY

You've shown me Heaven often . . .
For nothing else can soften
Like a baby's smile

Nothing else can go so deep
You know that Heaven surely weeps
Little baby tears

With those little arms outstretched
They bring out all your tenderness
A little baby's charms

No wonder Christ wants all of these
For they're the ones who want to please
Christ and you and me!

June 1980

YOU ARE A MOTHER

You've had your lovely baby, Dear
You'll love and protect and dry each tear . . .
For YOU ARE A MOTHER!

When they are old enough for those tumbles and falls,
You'll be their "Doctor" and answer their calls . . .
For YOU ARE A MOTHER!

When they go to school, they'll learn good and bad
You'll spank and protect them, even when you are sad . . .
For YOU ARE A MOTHER!

When they are dating and stay out too late,
You must discipline, without a Prudish state . . .
For YOU ARE A MOTHER!

When they marry, you are both happy and sad,
For they've entered a life you hope will be glad . . .
For YOU ARE A MOTHER!

When they have their children and come for advice,
You are happy within—won't have to think twice . . .
For YOU ARE A MOTHER!

When you are quite old and their time for you short,
They may even insist on an "Old Folks Resort" . . .
But you'll understand—For YOU ARE A MOTHER!

GOD IN ALL

Every little hill in a mountain
Every little wave in the sea
Every little sound of a rain drop
Brings back thoughts of you and me.

The beauty in each tiny little flower
The rareness of each snowflake that falls
The thought of a pearl in each oyster
Brings God into all both great or small

As the time comes for each expectant Mother
You hear the crying of her newborn babe
You can see the time and love that's been given
And you know another life has been saved!

January 21, 1984

BLESSINGS

The thunder clapped—
The lightning flashed—
As the rain came down
I know that God was blessing
This small, but friendly town.

Thanksgiving should be every day
But people don't recall
The blessings that "He" gives us
The great ones and the small.

Once again give thanks to God
For health and blessings too
He's there watching over us
In everything we do!

November 25, 1996

CONTEMPT VS. LOVE

Contempt breeds contempt—
As most of us know
But kindness brings love—
And gives us a glow!

If people would care—
They'd surely know God
For each single person
Should want to applaud!

When we're unkind
To the ones Undeserving—
It's surely not God,
The great One, we're serving!

The devil has hold—
Let's shake him free
And bring back God's love
For you and for me!

August 11, 1972

JUST A PRAYER

If we could stay, sweet Jesus,
Forever in Your arms
No complaint would we have
For we'd be safe from harm.

But with the chores You give us
We must be on our guard
The devil tempts those YOU love
We must pray very hard.

What's happened to this world, dear Lord?
Sin comes NOT from you
This human race, is a disgrace
Your example's not held true.

I'm told we're saints, sweet Jesus
Because we are Your friends
Please help us pray and do Your Will
From now until the end.

June 1980

SEAL OF FRIENDSHIP

We're filled with love, El Paso,
With your warmth and charm
The mountains that surround you
Keep us from much harm.

And Mexico so close to us,
(To some their language strange)
The opportunities we get,
Help our lives to rearrange.

The lovely customs and the music
And the graciousness we feel
Help to bring our nations close
And the bond of friendship seal!

December 8, 1980

KINDNESS

Kindness is needed all over the earth
Kindness was given to each at his birth
Why can't we retain this? We ask with a sigh
With each fleeting moment, it passes us by.

Greed seems to have taken the hearts of most men
And this surely leads to all kinds of sin
Prayer is what's needed all over the earth
That our hearts all return to the state of our birth

October 5, 1998

PLEASE

Each day I see how great You are
But You are up too high
If only I could see You
And Your heaven in the sky.

Dear God, I want so very much
To be a perfect wife.
A mother, too, and then to You
I dedicate my life.

Dear God, please always help me
I need you very much
I want to get to heaven
But I'm always in a rush.

So please help me remember
That heaven is my goal
Help me tread more slowly
And remind me of my soul.

No rushing through my prayers at night
No driving past the Church
And please be right there with me
At the final conscience search.

June 1980

JIM NANCE'S "SADIE"

The famed Jim Nance now is gone,
A legend he'll remain—
His precious Sadie stands alone,
She'll always be the same.

She stayed with him,
Through trial and tribulation
She waited patiently at home
While he would serve their nation.

Few great men have made it
Through adventure and through strife
Without, standing in their shadow,
A brave and model wife.

And this our gentle Sadie is,
No outcry will we hear
But one close look into her eyes
You'll see the held back tear.

The Rangers will miss this great, fine man
And other will miss him too;
But our kind and gentle Sadie Nance
Has his memory to see her through.

Jim died August 8, 1971
August 9, 1971

A FRIEND

We've shared each other's happiness
We've known each other's sorrow
Together we could whip our grief
And have a happier tomorrow.

Friends are terribly needed
In this great, sad world today
They'll give a nudge, quickly trudge
To see our humor on display.

Don't become a hermit
And think you're the only one
With troubles and with heartaches
For they number one by one.

God gave us all a cross to bear
But He also gave us friends
I hope that you'll remember this
When your day comes to an end.

If today has been quite hectic
Pull that sense of humor out
A quiet prayer, kind words to share
You'll find peace without a doubt.

June 1980

THE SWEET OLD LADY

I know a sweet old lady,
So kind and cheerful, too,
It's really quite amazing
For there's nothing she can do!

She may be paralyzed these days,
But watch her twinkling glance
There are so many memories
When she never missed a dance.

People like to visit her
For she never is depressing
But with her very witty ways,
She often keeps them guessing.

I'm sure that you know someone, too,
Who's old and kind, and fond of you
Remember you'll be old someday——
Just hope that you'll be kind and gay.

Sweet and kind old people
Are the ones who help the young
Don't forget their praises
Always should be sung!

June 1980

WHAT IS REAL?

There are some you can't trust with a secret
Surely can't trust with your love!
When your heart's beating fast—don't look to the past.
You know that you're loved from above.

Good looks are often deceiving,
So are the words that they say,
Don't care who they hurt—they must come first,
They always want things their way.

They sound like they really love you,
And you fall under their spell.
But when you really need them,
It's out the door . . . "Farewell"

When your heart is breaking,
And you can't even smile
Just know that God is waiting,
He's been there all the while!

October 24, 1995

ETERNITY

Eternity's defined in so many ways,
It could mean distance—or so many days,
It could mean a heartbeat—the roar of a plane
It could mean kindness or a day to ordain.

When someone is angry and driving a car
Eternity means the distance you are—
From where you are going and how long it takes
Each heartbeat is felt when he hits the brakes.

The long days in college—the tests that arrive
Eternity means that you hope to survive
The hastening day—for your ordination
Your prayers that will help someone's salvation.

Eternity means the hours and days
When someone you love is so far away—
The minutes and seconds, until he is back
Into your arms for the love that you lack!

Compassion and kindness can mean so very much
To someone who's lonely and needing a touch—
Of a friendly smile, for their days have been long,
Eternity's passing with each word of a song!

June 6, 1973

SINS

We all sinned again today
Although we knew it wrong;
Our promises that are not kept
Are forgotten like a song.

Our God has been so patient
And forgiven us each time;
He sent His son down to earth
For sins like yours and mine.

January 9, 2000

PRAYER PROBLEMS

We always said our prayers at nite
And said the rosary often
Nothing else can help you out
Or make a hard heart soften

We all have problems every day
"Whatever shall we do?"
The devil is there pushing us
To make wrong choices (or be true)

Remember God is watching us
In everything we do
And our Guardian Angels
Are always with us, too!

May 25, 2002

RIGHTS OF THE ROAD

What change comes over people
When they step into the car
You would need imagination
To believe the change, by far!

That gentle little lady
Who speaks so soft and sweet
When she's behind the steering wheel
Look out! Get off the street!

The drinking buddies—arm in arm
Have just now left the bar
Friendship must stay on the street
When they get in the car.

"Rights" are what the teens want
Just like the dear old folk
But who gives "Rights" to others?
Now this is quite a joke.

Please don't become a lion
Or a tiger "by the tail"
Just remembering always, that
Someone's brakes could fail.

Remember when you're standing
And a life lies in the street
You will have a long, long time
To pray there's no repeat!

March 5, 1980

THOSE BULLETINS

Our li'l ole Church in the Valley
Has taken a lot of "guff"
Including the ole' church bulletin
Which really has it rough

The time it takes to type it up
Is not believed by some
And those who do believe it
Seem to have "forgotten one."

It takes a day to run it off
And folding comes in, too,
But the phone still is ringing
Cause they "don't know what to do!"

June 1980

SANCTIFYING GRACE

Gifts can come from people
Everyone knows this . . .
But gifts that come from Heaven
Bring eternal bliss.

The dignity that God reflects
We surely must keep pure
As we want to be God's children
And make our Heaven sure.

June 1980

GRANDMA

When I was just a little girl
We'd go to Grandma's house.
I remember being told . . .
"Be quiet as a mouse!"

"Children do not speak,
Unless they're spoken to."
(Today we do not think this rule
Should quite be held so true.)

We were put into the corner,
With our hands placed in our laps
We dared not to touch a thing
For fear we would be slapped.

But now that I'm a Grandma,
The young are thought of more
I'll give them all the love they want
To even up the score.

June 1980

GO TO HIM

When loneliness surrounds you
At the close of each day
There is only God to go to
He's waiting, He wants it this way.

God too wants to be needed
Go to Him, He'll hold out his hand
No matter what you are thinking
He's there, and He'll understand.

So when your heart is broken
Remember He'll know and see
He loves us all so very much
He wants us happy, you and me.

Go to Him each day on rising
Go to Him when things get tough
Don't forget each day to thank Him
Cause He's there when things are rough.

January 7, 1996

GRAZING TIME

The wind blew through the oak trees
Where the bees had made their nest
The cows grazed in the fields
Picking out the very best.

The dark clouds seemed to gather
Where the sun had shone so bright
Peace seemed to overshadow
Whether day, or dark of night.

God had made the elements
Before He made each man
But the secrets of the universe
Are not ours to understand.

He also gave intelligence
That each of us might learn
Ambition keeps us going
for the answers we do yearn.

The cows still are grazing
the birds still take to wing
But we, the most intelligent,
Have forgotten how to sing!

May 31, 1988

THANK HIM

The white clouds in the heavens
Were rolling with the wind
Blue sky in the background
Showed beauty for a blend.

How many people do not see
The love that God has shown
Through the centuries "He's" been there
To make "His" presence known.

Do many people thank "Him"
I do not think this so
Even with the blessings
That always see to flow.

Just try to remember
From whom all blessings come
You'll surely sleep with ease at night
Knowing where the grace is from!

August 17, 2002

A NARROW LINE

When we humans were created
Some things were not defined
It's hard from comprehension
Like the narrowness of a line.

Love and hate seem so opposite
And yet as many know
To be tortured when you love one
Can start seeds of hate to grow.

Or if you think you hate another
Not one good thing does show
Then suddenly you are needy
And it's that one who helps you so.

Don't ever think you're perfect
Cause we're all imperfect indeed
Try always to show kindness,
Help sow love by planting seed.

June 1980

GOD'S GENTLE RAIN

It was raining, oh so softly
When the wind began to blow
We needed rain so badly
As only God could know

If we put our lives within 'His' hands
For money, health or rain
We are doing what 'He' wants us to
with 'Him' we will remain.

When you push for just your will
You know it won't be good
But doing what our God would want
will shield us as it should.

March 28, 1999

TOMMY

He never did like poetry
He tries to hide his feelings
If sentiment should come in sight
Of any of his dealings.

He really does work very hard
And playing he does well
About his sports or college work
There is a lot to tell.

In marriage he did very well
For Audrey is his wife
And precious little Shannan
Will help complete his life.

If you think I'm proud of him
And prizes he has won—-
I'm sure that you have guessed by now
That Tommy is my son.

June 1980

JERRY

God knew what He was doing
When he made that boy of mine
He made him strong and healthy
And his looks were mighty fine!

He gave him quite a talent
For loving helpless ones—
He gave him much compassion
Even though he had been shunned!

He's good at putting things to working—
When others say, "no use!"
He loved all kinds of animals—
He couldn't stand abuse!

But most of all—he loved the old
Though others did forget
And with his heart so full of kindness
Life may be kind to him yet!

GOD'S LOVED ONES

Children are so special
God made them first, you see
Suddenly they're all grown up
Just like you and me.

When God gives us babies
It's like he gave us clay
He said that we must mold them
In a special way.

So many do not take the time
To do as we've been told
They selfishly withhold love
Which messes up the mold

Mary came to warn us
And remind us of God's love
God has sent his angels
To help us from above.

March 3, 1998

THE WAITING ROOM

The crowded doctor's office
Had many kinds to wait
Old ones, young ones
Wondering 'bout their fate.

A little baby crying
Old people talking loud
Young people in discussions
Some watching a rain cloud.

The receptionists stay busy
With all who come and go
But I guess that it's much better
Than a day that's just too slow.

We really need our doctors
And pray for them each day,
To stay well and care for us
So we can go our merry way!

March 20, 2001

OUR FUTURE

God leads doctors by the hand
In this, our "should be" Christian land.
"In God we trust" is our motto
Instead of church, we go to Lotto.

We've killed our future with abortion.
Instead of babies, we want fortune.
Can't anyone begin to see
The more we have, the less we're free?

Our precious babies, sorely missed,
By childless couples who now wish
They had had a family tree
With lots of kids like you and me!

Is this the way our country's gone?
Instead of love, we want song,
Instead of babies, we want money
Instead of work, some want honey.

Schools need prayer we must agree,
To have a future history.

July 23, 2000

MONSIGNOR BURNS

Each day I pray for those I love
And you are on that list
Close to the top, your name remains
On this I do insist.

Saintliness you do not claim
Though we think you rate high
Each of your words circle your head
Like a halo in the sky.

To speak of things we should know
And know your friends' concerns
Leaves just one special speaker——
Edward James Burns.

June 1980

JOHN PAUL II

I looked and saw a gentleman
In a long white robe
Upon his head a beanie—white
Which said he was the Pope.

A gentleness was on his face
And kindness filled his eyes
The words of wisdom that he spoke
To some, were a surprise.

Leaders of countries he could face
His dignity would reign
But with Christ's little children
A loving Father he became.

When I saw him kneel in prayer
A tear was in his eye
For he knew that upon him
Millions did rely.

June 1980

LOVE WISHES

He stood with his arms around her
He whispered sweet words in her ear
The music was playing loudly
His sweetness was all she could hear.

She wished the day could be over
And the night would be with them again.
She hoped he would always love her
And things would be back where they'd been.

THE BEAUTY SHOP

I sat looking at the ladies
It really was a sight
Some were tall and skinny
Others were just right.

Some were making faces
As funny as could be
Some were reading magazines
Or looking 'round—like me.

Some were very fidgety
Wishing they were through
Others sat there patiently
Without a thing to do.

When they leave, they're pretty
They can dance or hop
But I feel sorry for those ladies
Who run the beauty shop.

June 1980

LEGS

After I married and met some 'not-so-nice' women, who constantly talked about my 'ugly, fat legs'. I didn't even think of them until this one woman in particular liked to embarrass me in front of others.

When the kids started arriving and I had trouble with them swelling and with veins, the Doctors got in on it, too.

But my contention is—these are the legs God gave me and they just have to do until I die. Thank you, God, for giving me two!

LEGS

Those beautiful legs so shapely
On many women I see
Then I look down and really do frown,
These ugly legs are on me!

People do not realize
I wear slacks so "they" can hide
When swimming comes 'round, I won't be found,
I'll find a reason to stay inside.

I think about this often
I talk to the "Man" above.
God may have sent me ugly legs
But "He" sent me LOTS of love.

So I'll just keep my legs hidden
A secret they'll remain
As long as I keep my God in sight
There'll be no need to complain.

April 28, 2001

THANK YOU, LORD

My family doesn't care, Lord,
Or I'd have never strayed
Away from anyone of them
You know how hard I've prayed.

A vow against my wishes
Had started all of this
I needed to be cared for, Lord,
This was just my single wish.

Despair has come so many times
When I'd reach out to them
They'd turn away—as if to say
My usefulness had worn too thin.

In my thoughts, and in my prayers
You've finally made me see
No matter how I've hurt You
You are near and still love me.

Thank you, Lord.

June 1980

OFTEN

I've often watch the sun
Come rising in the sky

I've often watched an ant
Go busily passing by

I've smelled Your lovely flowers
So fresh and wet with dew

I've watched the many people
Flock into their pew

I've wondered how we sinners
Can be so evil still

When we know that it was You, Lord,
Who gave us our free will.

June 1980

CARRY ON

I stood looking out the window
Though my heart was in my hands
For intuition told me,
But I hoped I didn't understand.

The car had crashed——I felt the pain
Although I wasn't there
The crushed, torn bodies strewn about
Are the ones in life for which I care.

When the doorbell rang, I felt a chill
I tried so hard to pray
Then I faced a lone policeman
Who knew not a consoling word to say!

I tried to make it easier,
So he could soon be gone,
But as he spoke the words I knew
I wondered how I'd face each dawn.

The hardest thing in life, is living
When the ones you love are gone
There will always be more challenges
You must smile and carry on!

June 1980

POPCORN

The aroma was delicious—
As we walked into the store
The popcorn was a' poppin'
Behind that small closed door.

Little people think so fast
And move faster even more
The little fellow reached right up
And let it tumble on the floor.

The salesgirl just stood lookin'
She knew not what to do—
The manager was livid
You'd swear he had turned blue.

The little fellow wasn't bothered
Til his mother turned around
Then he saw her face was red
He soon let out a howling sound.

The popcorn still smells luscious
But the doors don't close the same
For they put in a new window
And a brand new cushioned frame.

June 1980

MY VALENTINE

A valentine sent each day
Is not enough to convey
How much I love you!

Though the day comes once a year
I wish that you could plainly hear
How much I love you!

No words I know can describe
My feelings that go deep inside
How much I love you!

I still cannot hear or see
The words you're in love with me . . .
But still I love you!

June 1980

THINK ABOUT IT . . .

The best way for nations to do away with War
Is to Pray More and Prey Less

Diplomacy is letting someone else have your way.

Never fear that life shall come to an end,
But rather fear it shall never have a beginning.

Why is it, people with the most sympathy
Often waste it on themselves?

If we took the bad language out of today's movies
We'd go back to silent films!

To be seventy years young is more hopeful
Thank to be forty years old.

MY LOVE

Of all the traits he does possess
There isn't a single one bad
To know him means warmth, to see him, joy
A thought of him makes me glad.

I didn't know love could go so deep
Even when we're far apart
I can see his face smiling down at me
His smile goes right to my heart

Though I'll see him no more—the love will remain
But no one will know that it's there
I'll smile and act gay, just don't look my way
If a tear should slip through my stare.

I know love means pain, must it always be so
Just because we were wrong from the start
Our feelings must hide—we'd be crucified
From our duties we cannot part.

I'll go on through life and my duties fulfill
Hoping somewhere in life we will meet
But my heart cannot take many more blows
Just look down, Love, my heart's at your feet.

June 1980

HE ISN'T YOU

To and from the dance floor
You've only held my hand
Yet when I think of you
We've been to Lover's Land.

This is all so silly
To the young, I'm very old
One day soon they'll feel this way
But now they can't be told.

You don't even know you've done it
You've touched my heart, my sweet,
Please be careful where you walk
My heart's there at your feet.

I know you love another
Someone cares for me, too
But how can I care for him
When I know he isn't you!

February 16, 1996

NEEDS

Everyone needs to be needed
No matter their station in life
Whether the man of the family
Or the shy little stay-at-home wife.

From infancy on, you'll have problems
And balance will come with our needs
A student, a teacher, policeman,
All will be known by their deeds.

If only we'd smile at our problems
A laugh is much nicer than tears
We'd soon have a world to be proud of
We'd have God back, instead of our fears.

June 1980

SUNDAY MORNING

"Thou keep holy the Lord's day"
This command was given
But excuses come from every side
The devil's thoughts are driven
Into the hearts of men!

God has done so much for us
And men have done so little
Accomplishments we seem to like
Are done to Satan's fiddle
Fickle hearts of men!

"Church is full of hypocrites"
This excuse we hear
But do they ever pray to God—
Now would that be sincere?
Say the lips of men!

When our lives are over
And some are down in hell
They'll spend their time remembering
That lovely old Church bell . . .
Too late for sorrow!

December 9, 1979

THE MOUNTAINS

The mountains seem so scary, if
They're steep and brakes are bad
But if you are just watching
They could not make you sad.

The beauty in descending
Breath-taking as can be
You feel you are in Heaven
With all the world to see.

I've always loved the mountains
I feel they are God's home
When I die, He'll take me there
Forever more to roam.

June 1980

THE CHRISTIAN WAY

When Christ lived upon this earth
He surely left a sample—
That all of us should Christians be,
And follow His example!

How can any people say
That God indeed is dead?
Did He not show His love for us
By allowing His blood to be shed?

Then Easter Sunday morning came,
He had risen from His grave—
And still they did not understand
All this was for our souls to save!

God still loves and watches us,
He's done all that He can do—
If we'd use the Grace He gives,
We'd save our souls and others, too!

ST. PATRICK'S DAY

St. Patrick's Day is coming
It's a special day for me
My people always danced and sang
I joined in when I was three.

That was a special "party day"
The music there was great
The food was fine, drink flowed like wine,
Gaelic was spoken on that date.

Most of my people now are gone
But memories cannot be taken
No matter the problems in the world
Irish love is not forsaken.

March 3, 1996

EACH DAY I PRAY

I know I'm nothing special
But please, dear Lord, I pray
Make me kind and gentle
As I go from day to day.

You've sent me lots of chores to do
And I'd like to do them right
To love, appreciate and guide,
To teach our young to pray each night.

You surely have been good to me
I'll give you thanks each day
Just help me guide these young ones
And keep them on the path—Your way!

June 1980

DID'JA

Did'ja ever watch a one year old?
They're cute as they can be
They're little dolls—girls or boys
So soft and cuddly.

They toddle here, they get in there,
The things you want—they reach
They're really great explorers
There's much that you must teach.

Did'ja ever watch a two year old?
Now this is quite a stage
They're conquered walk, they're trying talk
There's much for this young age.

Did'ja ever watch a three year old?
My favorite age is this—
They walk, they talk, they imitate
They bribe you with a kiss.

They follow here, they follow there,
And questions seem to flow
When you stop to answer them,
They'll wide-eyed say, "I know!"

Did'ja ever stop and wonder
Or have a single doubt
That God's love and little babies
Are what life's really all about—

Did'Ja?

June 1980

COMPASSION

On us You have compassion
You've had it all along
You've loved us and You've watched us
Even when You knew us wrong.

It's a pity we can't see You
For You're right before our eyes
But we humans are so selfish
And it's lust that hypnotizes.

The few who are so faithful
Will triumph in the end—
They have known all along
You were their One, True Friend.

June 1980

NATURE

No matter where you go
No matter what you do
God's handiwork's all 'round us
But we just look "right through!"

We never see the sky
Or the beauty of the day
We rarely see the flowers or trees
We just go our "busy way."

One day when we're too old
To do our "busy things"
We'll wonder how we missed all this
Nature sounds and birds who sing.

October 26, 1979

JELLY-N-ME

I was expecting my 8th child when I wrote this one and I think it's still most of my kids favorite. All of this happened in one day.

Back then, we used cloth napkins and tablecloths. We also 'dressed up' to go anywhere—the store, to town and especially to church. You didn't even think about having to check the seat of the chair before sitting.

The rest is explained in the poem.

JELLY-N-ME

Here I am 'a fussin'
Once again today
And there are all my children
Sleeping after play.

The day has finally ended
And I am so relieved
I'm sure that only God can know
The thoughts that I've conceived.

There was jelly on the tablecloth
(To start my "perfect" day)
There was jelly on a chair
(I had asked a friend to stay).

I dressed to do my shopping
And what else would appear?
But a gooey jelly sandwich
Spread upon me by a "Dear".

I went to say the rosary
And stuck to every bead
With little eyes upon me, saying:
"Won't you take the lead?"

When you stop and think about it
There's no cause for great alarm
How can little jelly-eaters
Really do a lot of harm?

So now with this behind me
And I'm calm as I can be
I know that jelly was surely made
For Mothers just like me.

June 1980

TIME

Time is a commodity
That cannot be replaced
It's like a written secret
That's gone when it's erased.

Time is very valuable
With money, can't be bought
But to those who love you
Your time is always sought.

Please do not waste it,
For God will ask you "Why?"
You wasted something precious
Before your day to die.

November 15, 1979

THANKSGIVING

If we'd not had this family
My food would be "Gourmet"
Instead of wealth—we have health
And many thanks to say . . .

I thank my God for babies . . .
As innocent as can be!
I thank my God for all the love
That He has given me.

I thank my God for each new day
The air, of which we breathe!
I thank God for the happiness
In marriage that we see.

I thank God for Un happiness . . .
For that comes often too
It helps to make us realize
The wrong things that we do.

But most of all—I thank my God
For sending us His son
And for all of the forgiving
For us that He has won!

I hope that I shall not forget
In any days to come . . .
To take time out and thank my God
For all that He has done.

1971

INSTEAD

Why is it so easy
To say bad instead of good?
It would be much nicer
to speak kindly as we should.

Christ said to turn the other cheek
Instead we wag the tongue
Instead of speaking from the heart
Bad thoughts and words are often sung.

Everyone has nice points
But we see only bad
Humanity has lost its path
And this is very sad.

So stop and check on you today
Your faults will go past seven
Find only good to talk about
You'll find your way to heaven.

February 8, 1977

MY DOG PENNY

I've had her for 10 years or more
She's loyal as can be
If I cried or had "bad luck"
She'd try hard to comfort me.

I told her many secrets
She never did betray
All she wanted was some love
Her eyes had this to say.

If strangers came, she barked at them
She didn't leave my side
She waited to see how I'd act
Before she'd be their guide.

If only humans would be this kind
And be helpful to one another
Things would be the way God wants
Loving family and each other.

May 18, 1996

NO ONE

No one but God knows our secrets
No one but God knows our pain
If only we'd pray—instead of curse
When we feel we're going insane

You can't pull and push together
They must be done separately
Instead of just rush—and—causing a fuss
Take your time and you're apt to agree

May 5, 1996

GOD'S HELPERS

A saint is the person who'll listen
At night or brightest of day
A saint is the one who will help you
Even when you insist on 'your way!'

A saint will overlook rudeness
Whether it's a spouse or another
A saint will try to see goodness
In a stranger, a Mom, or a brother.

When you're in an unknown city
And cannot find your street
A saint will help you in your find
And make your plans complete.

A saint will never forget our God
He knows who's in command
Whether he's close to home or in
A far away foreign land.

April 12, 1992

A PRAYER

My Jesus, My Jesus
I must do Your Will—
I know I've sinned
But I love You still!

I need Your strength
I need Your love
I need all of the help
I can get from above!

You're kind and forgiving
No matter the sin
This sorrowful sinner
Begs forgiveness again!

December 1973

OMA

I'm just another Grandmother
(There really are a lot)
But no one else could give the love
Just like our children got.

Our own have grown so very much
For "wee ones" we do yearn
But Lord have mercy on us
They have energy to burn.

Some are sweet and lovable
Some are very serious
A few of them cry a lot.
Some laugh 'til they're delirious

But all of them are precious
And sweet as they can be
And each of them say "Oma"
To a picture, just like me.

June 1980

LUCKY ME

Dear God, You've made me lucky,
And happy as can be—
You took the ones I care about
And gave them back to me!

There was misunderstanding
Which all could lead to sin—
But You're so great—You made things clear,
And brought us back again!

There is much misunderstanding
And strife throughout our land
If all would turn back to You—
No nation against us could ever stand!

THE RIGHTS OF OTHERS

What change comes over people
when they step into the car?
You would need imagination
to believe the change, by far!

That gentle little lady
who speaks so soft and sweet
When she's behind the steering wheel
Look out! Get off the street.

The drinking buddies—arm to arm
have just now left the bar.
Friendship must stay on the street
when they get in the car!

"Rights" are what the teen want
just like the dear old folk
But who gives "rights" to others
now this is quite a joke!

Please don't become a lion
Or a tiger "by the tail"
Just remember always, that
Someone's brakes could fail.

Remember when you're standing
and a life lies in the street
You will have a long, long time
to pray there's no repeat.

GEORGE WEST

George West's pride is her people
All are basically fine
Some stand taller than others
This is no worry of mine.

Our hearts are really what matters
No matter the time of the year
If you've gone to church on Sunday
Or a ball game without any fear.

We have confidence in our players
Whether they win or lose
We've known most since tiny babies
And our caring is part of their dues.

Some of us like to go dancing
Some like a party at eight.
Games are often suggested
Whether alone, or with a date.

Everyone's always invited
That's the rule you see
Whether a game or story fest
Togetherness is great you'll agree.

December 15, 1995

A DAUGHTER

The Mother, so sad, stood silent
Praying her tears wouldn't show
Her daughter soon would be leaving
In the car that stood below.

The lovely daughter was pregnant
Frightened and feeling alone
She felt that she must leave this
Place—always she'd called home.

The love and emotions running high
Were close between these two
But the young needs time to understand
Some of the things they do.

A young life soon would be coming
In four months it was bound to appear
Then this daughter would learn first-hand
Of heartbreak and true Mother's tears.

April 19, 1979

ALBERT

My darling little grandson
As I hold you in my arms
Your little eyes look up at me
You know you're safe from harm.

You are so very tiny now,
Who knows what lies ahead?
You were blessed with much love
And many prayers were said.

Always love your Mother
She went through much for you
Let not one man harm her
Be careful what you do.

October 22, 1979

THE END

Goodbye sounds so final
It's better to say it now
We both knew it was coming
We just weren't sure how.

How many times have I told you
I won't see you any more
When I think it's over
You're there at my front door.

You thought you cared for another
Until you entered my life
I won't sit around waiting
While you decide who'll be your wife.

This "farewell" is final
My life will turn out fine
With my family and religion
You'd be at the end of the line.

March 3, 1996

GOSSIP

Some folks think it's funny
And many take delight
In listening to gossip
Whether near or out of sight.

You'd think it was elastic
The way the truth is stretched
To find the true details
You'd need an artist and a sketch.

You wouldn't be so eager
To listen to those lies
If it were you "they" talk about
You'd want to swat those "flies."

Never repeat gossip
Or even listen in—
You're sure to regret any words
When it's *Your* name linked with sin.

January 29, 1996

YOUR WAY

All I want and need is love
I'm sure that you do, too
You know by now, I'm not complete
When all I want is you.

Will you be there by my side
When I am very old
You know all the happenings
The stories to be told.

When we're together
To the music we do sway
Let's take it nice and easy
Things will go your way.

February 25, 1996

THE DANCE FLOOR

I must put up my dancing shoes
My feet are full of pain
It breaks my heart to stay at home
Only the memories will remain.

My heart is full of music
How can I stay in a chair?
With dancing all around me
I want to be right out there.

My doctor is a good one
With time he'll fix my feet
Then I'll return to the dance floor
And my life will be complete.

February 27, 1996

MY ANGEL "BUTCH"

What's your name, My Angel?
I'd really like to know
You must be with me always
And go everywhere I go.

I'd like to know you better
You were sent to be my guide
I guess that you are stuck with me
I know you're here, by my side.

Trouble seems to follow me
No matter where I go
You so often shake your heard
Do I hear when you say "No"?

I'm just gonna call you "Butch"
Until I know your name
Remembering you'll stay with me
Until at death my soul you'll claim.

August 7, 1975

SMILE

A smile is something special
A smile is always free
A smile can chase the blues away
And it makes all sadness flee.

A smile is so worth giving
To all of those in need
A smile can make contentment grow
It's much like the mustard seed.

A smile helps when you're weary
Or when you need a friend
A smile's so very worth our while
It helps bring triumph in the end.

June 1980

MY "DANNY BOY"

I loved the song "Oh, Danny Boy"
I waited many years
But God is good and after awhile
My "Danny Boy" appeared.

He filled the bill in every way
So precious and so sweet
With three young babes and "Danny Boy"
I thought my life complete.

But God knows best and soon
He sent—7 in a row
With all these youths, our happiness
Was surely bound to grow.

My "Danny Boy" is now grown up
At least, he's on his way
I hope and pray his character
Stay as it is today.

One day, I know my "Danny Boy"
Will fill me with more pride
And beaming with a Mother's heart
My face I'll never hide.

One day more distant than we know
In Heaven we will meet
I'll say, "I loved my 'Danny Boy'
He made my life complete."

June 1980

LOVE IS IMPORTANT

How many people realize
(Or should I say how few?)
That love's the most important thing
In all we say and do!

Our prison's full of people
Who didn't have much love,
The lack of it has made them hard—
(Too late to send a peaceful dove!)

Our teenagers who are rebellious
Can't really understand
If they'd had love and discipline
There'd be no reason to lift a hand!

Our very young are learning
And coming up so fast—
They surely must have the love they need
Before their future's cast.

Love and Charity are the same—
But many do not know,
How important it is to understand
They need love to help them grow!

I LOVE YOU, JESUS

I love you, sweet Jesus
Please let me be yours

I want to be with you
But can't close the door—

To this life that I'm living
Right here on this earth

It's your choice for our dying,
Just like at our birth!

I'm anxiously waiting
For your beck and call

I pray that I'm ready
Please don't let me fall!

October 20, 1979

THE WHITE CLOUDS

The white clouds are so lovely
As we drive these many miles
It seems that God is painting
Pictures for His files

We saw Peanut's Snoopy
Running 'cross the sky—
And there's a big ol'e eagle
And a sail boat passing by.

We saw God's hand extended
To give us more, you see,
But with the wind, it disappeared
Leaving just a memory.

God gives us all so very much
Our lives, our loves and more
Imagination's right there, too,
It evens up the score.

May 31, 2000

HAROLD

Harold is a kind man
He's sweet and loving too
As far as our religion
He thinks the way I do.

He never had a sister
But he had a kindly wife
Who gave him three fine children
And helped fulfill his life.

All humans will have problems
That's part of life, you see
But knowing God is watching
Is helping you and me.

Companionship is what we need
The longer that we live
Love helps even memory loss
And we just take and give.

Loving Harold comes easy
There isn't any strife
I hope and pray I'll always be
A good and loving wife!

March 11, 1998

MEMORY OF ALZHEIMER'S

Sitting in the Nursing Hoke
Wondering how he'd be
Would he remember or
Even think of me?

Each day he is much different
Sometimes as sweet as pie.
Some days he knows me
Other days—I don't know why.

But I know he's "in there"
And God knows him too.
All I can do is wait for him
And see what he will do.

No matter when God calls us
At night or in the day.
We will be ready
'Cause we know that it's His way.

June 14, 2008

LONELY OR BLUE

Some people talk when they're lonely
Some people talk when they're blue
Some people talk just to be talking
And they don't know what else to do.

I know I sing when I'm happy
I sometimes sing when I'm blue
I sing to tell God I love Him
I hope that you do too!

May 1, 2001

A PRIEST

A Priest will hear confessions
When a ballgame's being played
And there's old "Chatty Hanna"
To make sure he's delayed.

A Priest keeps his appointments
To make sure things run smooth . . .
But the person in the Parish
Thinks his time is "ours" to use!

He may not look just like a Saint
For he is human, too,
He's given up all earthly things
To help save me and you!

June 1980

A COWBOY

I know and love a cowboy,
Who's sweet as he can be
Everyone seems to love him,
I guess I'm lucky he likes me.

Even the cows love him,
They "Moo" for him each day.
He'll go out and feed them,
And send them on their way.

He plants and weeds his garden,
Then gives the food away.
He's there when others need him,
What more is there to say?

When his wife was living,
He was loyal as could be.
He's still a loving father,
Ask his daughter, you will see.

"Everyone loves a Cowboy"
I've heard this many times.
Even in the songs they write,
When everything must rhyme.

November 1, 1998

THE UNUSED RULE

"You must think before you speak"
This I learned in school
But who'd a'guessed from what I say
I'd ever heard this rule.

My biggest trouble is my mouth
I speak before I plan
Embarrassment is oft' the case
'Tween me and fellow man.

Praying helps in all you do
So make your mouth a prayer
This way you'll know what you say
Always will be fair.

October 18, 1994

WHITE-CLOTHED NUNS

I came from sedation quite slowly
Almost like life'd just begun
And who was standing beside me?
A beautiful white-clothed Nun.

Through illness and convalescence,
They'll be at your side in a blink
With comforting words, a pat on the back
A sweet and sly little wink.

I know that the medicine's healing
And our brilliant Doctors are grand
But I'd like to build a pedestal
Where our white-clothed Nuns should stand.

June 1980

SLEEPLESS NIGHTS

Why can't I go to sleep these nights
I really know the answer
It's because of you, my sweet,
My best and favorite dancer.

You are always in my thoughts
If asleep or wide awake
I always want to reach for you
And pray there's no mistake.

I never want to lose you
But you really aren't mine
I close my eyes and pretend
This way it works out fine.

All I want or need is love
What am I to do?
I'm sure that you know by now
The love I want is You.

February 20, 1996

WANT

I want a man who's all dressed up
In shirt and coat and tie
His manners be impeccable
His eyes blue as the sky.

He will hold the door for me
If we kiss, he'll tip his hat
Kind words must flow naturally
What do you think of that?

Instead I fell for you, my sweet,
No coat, no hat, no tie.
As we dance to the music
I feel we're floating in the sky.

I'm sure that I'm not what you dreamed
Or wanted all along
But when we are together
We create quite a song.

February 25, 1996

T.V.

In this, our generation
Radio's almost gone
So is imagination
But TV's on 'til dawn.

You're blurry-eyed next morning
Can't remember what you saw
But it must've been entertaining
For the attention it could draw.

The thing that aggravates you
There's a murder mystery on
The scene is now "Who done it?"
The commercials now come on.

They advertise food that'll make you fatter
Then talk about the waist
You don't know which to think about
But it's food that has the taste.

The beautiful maid is running
With the Indians closing in
But do they ever catch her?
The commercials on again.

Scientists say it's much better
Than radio could ever be
But our good imagination's gone
Cause of commercials and TV.

June 1952

THE OLD FASHIONED CLOTHESLINE

Most of my days were spent at the clothes line when the kids were young. Those 'throw away' diapers were not even thought of until my last two were here and their skin was so sensitive they would break out if I put them on my babies.

My soft white skin turned beige from sun burn while hanging clothes on the clothesline.

THE OLD FASHIONED CLOTHESLINE

Clotheslines are old fashioned
(As many people say)
I guess that I'm old fashioned—-
I kinda like it that way.

Women sit around and fuss
Because they're getting fat
But would they hang the clothes out—
Why who'd be caught at that?

There are so many problems
The answers we can't find
If they'd go to the clothesline
To their God they could unwind.

The breathing problems many have
Could sure be helped a lot
By the fresh air at the clothesline
T'would be free—it can't be bought.

So lose some fat and some small problems
And help your breathing, too,
Don't be afraid to be old-fashioned
It could be nice for you.

June 1948

A WORKING MOTHER

I stood hanging clothes on the clothesline—
(Though this is old-fashioned, I know)
Some may think of housework as dreary
But to me, it brings a warm glow!

The smelly socks all need washing,
There are papers strewn about—
The sink is full of dishes,
But I'll clean it all—they have not doubt!

I'd like to keep my house tidy,
All nice and neat and clean—
But now I am a working Mother,
Too tired to fit in my scheme!

I hope my work won't last too long,
So I can be home where I belong,
To clean our house and iron our clothes
And work out problems with a song.

Money is so useless
It's character that counts
And Mother needs to be there—
When children problems seem to mount!

Guess what! I think I'm quitting—
For what else can I do?
My family really needs me,
And to God's plan I must be true!

June 1973

DADDY

A Daddy is a special man—
Any male can "father"
A Daddy's there through thick and thin
Some "fathers" wouldn't bother.

A Daddy will give up a game
That he's looked forward to—
Because of little "Johnny's" needs
He knows that it's his due.

When the kids have left their home
And Daddy has grown old
Loving thoughts and memories
Always will be told.

October 11, 1980

A LETTER TO JESUS

June 6, 2007

When you go to church to visit, to pray, for whatever reason, you know that God is there in your mind and in the Tabernacle.

The 'Stations of the Cross' was something I used to pray every Friday. I couldn't keep from crying sometimes. That is why I wrote this poem.

A LETTER TO JESUS

Dear sweet Jesus,

Please understand—
I want to be with you and then kiss your hand—
A hand that was cruelly hurt and then nailed
To a cross on the hilltop because I had failed.

To keep your commandments the Father had said
Must be followed always and the path you had led.

Your life on this earth was so terribly hard
By the time you had died, your body was scarred
The beatings and torture of these mortal men
Yet you took it gladly because of all sin.

Heaven must be very sweet—
Please save me a spot there right at your feet.

June 6, 2001

HOLY INNOCENTS

Of all the stories that I've read
That touched my heart so deep
The precious "Holy Innocents"
Would really make me weep.

Those darling little babies
A whole life time ahead
Because of one man's jealousy
The streets all ran "blood" red!

But is there any difference
Between "those days" and now?
Our precious "Holy Innocents"
Still die—but can't say how.

Abortion is no different—
A precious life is lost
With our selfish thoughtlessness
Another life will be the cost.

December 16, 1981

AN ABORTION

May 28, 2007

During the time I was working with the kids on drugs, I also had kids "in trouble" coming to me. One young couple, I knew the boy and his family since he was tiny. He asked me not to tell his folk about the pregnancy. I didn't have to—her mother found out and forced her to have an abortion over in Mexico.

I wrote this poem as if I were the baby—I knew them well by this time and I was broken hearted to have to see and watch the girl suffer over the loss of her baby and "the father". The girl's mother had forbidden them to see each other. Whenever either one could, they'd sneak over to talk to me. But since I was still holding a real job, I didn't have the time I would have to liked to spend with them or any of the 'kids'.

Believe me, I was worn down completely. By the end of August I got a meeting between the kids and the police. I had promised the kids if they'd go, they would not have to go in police cars. I got as many car owners as I could, including mine, of course, but there were still 9 or 10 that I couldn't take.

The meeting started slowly, but 'snow-balled' soon. The kids asked the police questions and vice versa. It was a huge success.

AN ABORTION

Dear Lord, why did they do it?
I would have loved to live
Now I shall never know the joy
Of love that parents give.

My mother really loved my dad
That's why I almost came
But her mom wouldn't believe their love
She said "T'was just a game."

She took Mom to a Doctor
(But not a well-known one)
She said it would be scandalous
If "it" had not been done.

My mother sits and cries each day
I know what's in her heart
For she still longs to hold me
But we are far apart.

I think my Granny knows now
The wrong that she has done
She needs so much forgiveness
And mother's love re-won.

She really would have loved me
If she had let me live
I'd look just like my mother did
And had so much to give.

* * *

The many millions of "us"
Are worth more than a fortune
But they shall never know our love
For we each are "An Abortion"!

June 1970

A WIFE

A wife is NOT just a woman
Or there for a lustful thought
She is gentle, kind and loving
Doing what Jesus has taught

When 'love' brought them together
They had not a single care
So much was there ahead of them
With life and love to share.

If God sends them children
Each is taken as a gift
Thanks are sent toward heaven
With our prayers, our thanks do lift.

September 2, 2002

WEDDING BELLS

We were married on the same day
My granddaughter and me
We had chosen special fellows
On this we do agree.

It mattered not that they were young
Our age said we were old
What matters is what's in your heart
Of this I have been told.

As long as God is in our lives
Things can't go very wrong
Pray each day and go His way
You will find that you are strong.

June 20, 1999

IF HUSBANDS *REALLY* WANT A HAPPY MARRIAGE

If Husbands Really Want a Happy Marriage . . .

1. Try kissing your wife—I mean kiss her—not just a dutiful peck.
2. Bring her an inexpensive gift occasionally—just because she "might like it."
3. Take her out to eat occasionally—just to break the monotony.
4. An occasional word of praise would help—don't just bark when things don't suit you.
5. If she looks bad—be tactful—let her know you appreciate all the times she looked great.
6. When you make love to her (and do it often) be gentle and not just for your own satisfaction.
7. DO NOT ridicule her in front of the children and constantly tell them her faults.
8. Don't side with the neighbors against your wife—remember she has a side, too.
9. Try cooperating when the children are given chores. The wife can't do everything. God wants us to train them—they'll be adults some day, too.
10. Be understanding, instead of critical, when your wife is upset or moody. She may be just deeply hurt and it's usually your fault—intentional or not!

MY DARLING EILEEN

My darling Eileen, so precious, so fair
No one on this earth could ever compare
With your wit and charm, showing so clear
Your two precious children had no need to fear.

You're there when needed,
by family or friend
Even to *Unknown*,
your time will you lend.

The day that God calls you—
You will be ready
Even "He" knows
that you're straight and steady.

April 1, 2001

ELLEN

God made this tiny little girl
And shined her like a lovely pearl
Then He sent her down to me—-
A lovely gift for this family

Her hair is red, her eyes are blue
Her dimple deep, her smile so true
A "gift" like this, only God can make
So flawless, so perfect, without mistake.

Born on December 3, 1959
Written December 6, 1959

CARRIE

Carrie is a darlin'
And sweet as she can be
She loves her Mom & Daddy
And still has love for me!

She has two handsome brothers
And one sister too—
God is always with her
To Him she's always true.

Even when life is very hard
She knows God's with her still
Praying's what we all must do
To fill our hearts, not our will.

When her life is over
And she sees the "Pearly Gate"
Our Lord will then reach out to her
With His love which is her fate.

May 20, 2002

GRANDFATHER

Grandfathers, too, were made by God
Just like all the rest
In your Grandfather Tom, I hope you know
You surely got the best.

He had to learn all by himself
(Wisdom takes so long)
For by the time you have it
A crisis has often gone.

But he went on, even when
Mistakes had come so high
No one could ever say at times
His loyalty would die.

I stood back and watched him
Even when discouragement came
And in his love, I finally saw
That he had stayed the same.

God has been so good to you,
Just like He has to me
Take your time and look around
No better grandfather will you see.

June 1980

THE WRONG HAND

When you are right handed
and you break your right arm
You say to yourself
"Can't do too much harm."
Then when you go to the table to eat
You miss your mouth and the food's at your feet.

A left hand comb never looks good
the hair won't lay down or look like it should
even a sandwich isn't the same
it's there to be eaten but looks very lame
the mayo that's there is not evenly spread
the meat and contents are not graciously fed.

My clothes are all crooked—
No makeup I wear
One look at me would give you a scare

Some day in the future
I will be well and we'll all sit and
laugh at the tales I'll tell!

February 23, 2003

THOSE MOTHBALLS

Being afraid of mice and bugs
I didn't use much logic
I sprinkled mothballs everywhere
I didn't know them toxic.

The mice and bugs stayed away
And mosquitoes dare not come
Friends and family went their way
The odor was too strong for some.

A young boy came to see Eileen
Ten minutes and he was gone
His mother made him strip and bathe
Because the odor lingered on.

It's been three long years since I've used them
And friends come to the door
they take a 'whiff' before coming in
They remember how it had been before.

April 18, 2000

GRANDPA'S HANDS

His large rough hands were gentle
As he reached down for the child
Even though he smelled from work,
She knew him sweet and mild.

All the children loved him—
To him they all would race
Just to see what Grandpa brought
And see his kindly face.

He's been gone for many years now,
But his memory's like a band
Everyone remembers him—
But mostly "Grandpa's Hands!"

May 26, 2001

ALL NIGHT ADORATION

H ouse of God, with a welcome mat,

I s so quiet—just one Nun sat—

S peaking to her Maker!

H e, who came from Heaven above,

O pened up a Heart of Love—

U seless as we all might be

S till He hopes that we might see

E ventual salvation!

June 1980

YOU

As each ray of sun beams
shine through the curtained lace
I look and see the one I love
and a smile is on your face.

If I stay within the house
to clean and wash, and bake,
Would you sit and talk with me and
like the taste of each new cake?

Or if I should go shopping
and chance to see a dress
I want so much to see your face
Your eyes would tell me "no" or "yes"!

No matter what I'm doing
and the phone should ring
My heart will surely skip a beat
I only hope your voice t'will bring!

At the close of every day
to God I always pray
Your name is first upon the list
of the many that I say.

You're even in my dreams, Dear.
You're with me night and day
Whether you are close to me
or out of town and far away.

June 1970

ANTICIPATION

Looking ahead for something
I'm sure we all would agree
T'would keep us going
If expensive, or just something free

Some place more value on money
Others, the feelings of heart
Our time is really of value
Unnoticed by those not too smart.

The word "love" has lost its meaning
Christ proved this when He came to earth
Down to this land of the greedy
Where poverty showed at His birth

Please, God, let us look at Christmas
Not for the gifts that it brings
But the thought of the "Babe" in the manger
Should daily make our hearts sing.

December 22, 1979

MY HUSBAND

My darling husband—can't you see
How very much you mean to me?
I need your strength, I need your love,
That's why God blessed marriage from above!

I call to you and though you're there
your look at me is just a stare
You never see or feel my needs
You're far away, in thought and deeds.

Others have tried so very hard
To make me love them, and you discard
Can't anyone understand me now?
Though you don't care, I took a vow.

I feel so tired and very weak
I reach for you, but cannot speak,
To say the words hidden in my heart—-
To explain to you, I'm just not smart.

Oh Tom, I need you desperately,
Please come and really look at me
See the hurt I've tried to hide
Then maybe you'll stay by my side.

June 1980

'MY' GOD

Thanking my God comes easy
He's' in my every thought
I try to see good in others
This is what I was taught.

Each day slips by so quickly
I'm glad my God is near
He helps me make decisions
By whispering in my ear.

Some folks call God "Yahweh"
"Jehovah's" often heard
The many names my God is called
Can often be absurd.

Remember God is on 'our' side
He watches and He waits
To welcome us when we come
Inside the Pearly Gates!

August 15, 1995

WHAT TO DO

If you see an ugly woman
There isn't any doubt—
All 'ya gotta do is
Turn her inside out.

When there's a lot of work to do
But there isn't any time
Go fix up and look your best
Then serve a lot of wine.

If you have an appointment
You know that you'll be late
All 'ya gotta do is call
And change the date.

March 5, 1999

HE LOVED ME ANYWAY

He's gone I know and I miss him
I needed love but I pushed him away
Why must we always learn too late
The hurtful things we often say.

Refrain:

       I tried hard not to love him
       His faults were easy to see
But hey, I'm no saint and he knew this
       But he loved me anyway.

Actions will always speak for you
       And they really do convey
Your thoughts, feelings, emotions
       Yet you're loved anyway.

How can I live without him
And know that I hurt him so
A smile on my lips may fool some
But it's to him I want to go.

Don't listen to the words of others
       Just listen to your heart
What else can I say, to convey
       I'm just not very smart.

I learned too late how much I cared
But it hasn't helped my feelings
I'm so depressed I must confess
I've really considered leaving.

The years can't go by fast enough
I'll die a little each day
The stone on my grave will probably say:
"She loved him, but he went away."

January 5, 1996

DEATH IS BEAUTIFUL

Dear Lord, I'm going to die soon
You're the only One Who knows
Let's keep it just our secret
As the time will quickly go.

Why do people worry when
They know it's near their time?
We all will go eventually
I'm glad it's close to mine.

If you are good when you are living
Then death you need not fear
For Heaven will be waiting
And many who are dear.

Death is really beautiful
If people only knew
How much You want them near You
Good things they'd always do.

I'll see You soon, dear Jesus,
Find a special spot for me
Help those that I'm leaving
Not grieve, but Your Will see.

June 1980

Get Published, Inc!
Thorofare, NJ 08086
14 September 2009
BA2009257